How to Live with a Huge Penis

HOW TO LIVE WITH

— A —

HUGE PENIS

ADVICE, MEDITATIONS, AND WISDOM FOR MEN WHO HAVE TOO MUCH

BY DR. RICHARD JACOB
& REV. OWEN THOMAS

QUIRK BOOKS

PHILADELPHIA

Library of Congress Cataloging in Publication Number: 2008936820
ISBN: 978-1-59474-306-1
Printed in the United States of America
Typeset in Sabon, Trade Gothic, and Trajan

Designed and illustrated by Doogie Horner
Production management by John J. McGurk

30 29 28 27 26 25 24

Quirk Books
215 Church Street
Philadelphia, PA 19106
quirkbooks.com

Contents

Recognize the symptoms of OMG

Fig. 1

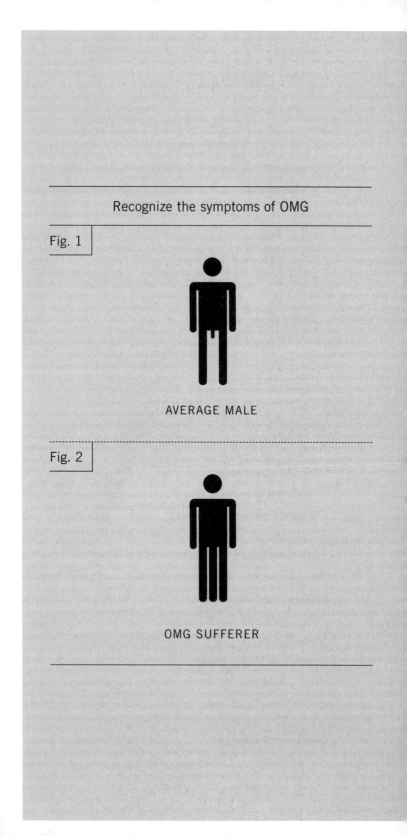

AVERAGE MALE

Fig. 2

OMG SUFFERER

Definition

OMG (Oversized Male Genitalia)

A genetic birth defect that causes the penis to grow absurdly large. The condition is thought to affect about 1 million American men, though that number may be artificially low due to underreporting. OMG is usually diagnosed between the ages of 12 and 14, although late-onset OMG has been reported in men as old as 25. There are currently no known causes or treatments and no known adverse physical effects; however, the condition is usually accompanied by serious psychological problems beginning in adolescence.

INTRODUCTION

The Secret Shame

Our society is obsessed with size, and "bigger" is almost always better. Men boast about driving the biggest truck. Hunting with the biggest rifle. Having the biggest biceps. Women pay thousands of dollars for bigger breasts. Movie posters exclaim "The Biggest Hit of the Summer!" and athletes live by the mantra "go big or go home." We love "bigger." "Bigger" is good. "Bigger" works.

But when it comes to penises, "bigger" is a curse. Something to be ashamed of. From a young age, boys with huge penises are taught to keep them locked away in the prison of their underwear. Mortified parents go to great lengths to keep the great lengths of their sons' genitals a secret, afraid they'll become the laughing stock of their supper clubs and church groups. While "normal" boys prance through locker rooms with their penises flopping gleefully about, snapping towels and comparing pubic manes, boys with OMG learn to feign other disabilities to avoid gym class altogether.

This pattern of avoidance continues into adulthood. Beaches, pool parties, and bike rides are just a few of the things that strike fear into the hearts of the over-hung. A man who carries a huge penis also carries a sack full of painful memories: being teased and physically attacked by schoolmates and co-workers. Accidentally making sexual partners hemorrhage or vomit. Suffering the sweltering days of summer in long pants.

Tragically, many men find it too much to bear. OMG sufferers have a suicide rate 30 times that of the average population. Many more express their pain through self-mutilation, often harming their penises or—in rare cases—cutting them off entirely.

I first met the Rev. Owen Thomas while I was

lying in a hospital bed in Cambridge, Massachusetts. He was the chaplain on call. I was the troubled young doctoral student who'd been found unconscious after beating my penis bloody with a hammer. I'd been courting a beautiful undergrad all semester, and, after a few dates, we found ourselves petting on my couch. But when I unzipped my fly and draped my penis on her leg, she let out a deafening scream and ran, half-naked, out of my apartment. In her panic, she fell down my building's staircase, broke her neck, and died instantly.

Over the next few months, while doctors worked to save my penis, Reverend Owen worked to save my soul. He taught me to see my condition as something that made me exceptional. "God's kicking your ass 'cuz he thinks you're man enough to take it," he was fond of saying. He also entrusted me with his own secret—that he, too, was afflicted with OMG.

Suffice it to say, I wouldn't be alive today without his love and wisdom.

Years later, with my own son about to start high school (happily, he inherited a tiny penis from my wife's side of the family), I felt a duty to spare other boys some of the pain that poisoned my life for so many years—to give them the tools to achieve the "normalcy" that took me so long to find. Reverend Owen and I have remained friends these long years, and I wouldn't have dreamt of writing this book without him.

So, in the name of healing and brotherhood . . .

—Dr. Richard Jacob
Sherman, Connecticut

Frequently Asked Questions About OMG

We'd like to begin by addressing the questions and concerns that most of the general public has about OMG. Dr. Richard and Rev. Owen will take turns answering.

Is someone with OMG technically a human being?
Dr. Richard: Yes, men with OMG have all the

same parts "normal" men do, not to mention all the same feelings. There's no scientific evidence to support some of the ugly anti-OMG myths that have persisted for generations, such as: "Men with OMG have small brains" or "Men with OMG eat babies."

Can I "catch" OMG from another person?

Rev. Owen: Absolutely not—and the stupidity of this question really pisses me off. How come everybody worries about "catching" a huge penis, but nobody ever says, "Oh, I hope I don't catch those enormous tits"?

Is OMG hereditary?

Dr. Richard: The short answer is, we think so. Getting funding for genetic research into OMG is difficult, since the general public would rather pretend the condition doesn't exist. But there have been several studies that show men with OMG are up to 80 percent more likely to have sons with OMG. Though we can't be absolutely sure, it's thought that one out of every 150 males is affected.

Am I required to register my OMG status with the government?

Dr. Richard: For many people, the answer (unfortunately) is still yes. The following four states still require men with an OMG diagnosis to register with their local police departments: Georgia, Tennessee, Mississippi, and Vermont. In Mississippi, police have the right to search your underwear during traffic stops if they suspect you're hiding a huge penis. In Vermont, OMG sufferers are required to have their penises photographed at the DMV.

Can women get OMG?

Rev. Owen: Can women have oversized male genitalia? Are you serious? I'm no egghead, but I think you need a penis to have a huge penis. True, there *is* a condition called OMFG (Oversized Mammaries and Female Genitalia), in which chicks get huge boobs and cavernous vaginas, but that's a hundred times rarer than OMG.

How long do men with OMG live?

Dr. Richard: Physically speaking, men with OMG have the same lifespan as the rest of the population. But the reality is, the psychological factors that accompany the disease (chiefly, depression and intense shame) lead many OMG sufferers to take their own lives. The best figures we have suggest that the average lifespan for an OMG sufferer is 51—a vast improvement over the average in the 1970s, which was 28.

Is having OMG the same thing as having a "French Bread"?

Rev. Owen: No. French Breads are long and skinny and don't count as OMG. Same with Tuna Cans, which are thick but short (see page 22 and glossary). You need a long, meaty pecker to be in the brotherhood.

CHAPTER

1

You Are Not Alone:
Huge Penises in History

*"Believe in yourself! Have faith in your
abilities! Without a humble but reasonable
confidence in your own powers you cannot
be successful or happy."*

—Norman Vincent Peale

As young OMG sufferers, we're taught to temper our expectations. Water down our dreams. Our parents tell us we'll never marry. Never have children. Never have a white-collar job because we can't wear slacks. Our high school guidance counselors tell us to keep to ourselves; hope for a quiet life of no more than 60 or 70 years. We're led to believe that the only big thing within our grasp is between our legs. But there are some men who have achieved huge things despite their huge penises. Your high school history textbooks probably didn't mention their OMG. But, the truth is, in front of every one of these great men was a great big penis.

Albert Einstein

A young Einstein once pondered how long it would take light to travel from one end of his gigantic penis to the other, a question that ultimately led to the Theory of Special Relativity. His most famous equation, $E = MC^2$, was also born of his battle with OMG. Einstein was struck by how much energy he spent lamenting the mass of his penis. "It was then that I realized that the process could be reversed—that a small amount of mass could be converted into a tremendous amount of energy!"

Benjamin Franklin

Many of Franklin's inventions were inspired by his enormous phallus, including the lightning rod and bifocals, which allowed him to see both the tip and the base of his penis at the same time. His giant member may have even saved America. In eighteenth-century France, huge penises were all the rage. Franklin used his own to great effect with the ladies of King Louis' court, who helped rally France to America's aid during the Revolutionary War.

Napoleon Bonaparte

It is one of history's great ironies that the term *Napoleonic complex* has come to mean a need to prove oneself because of short stature. In fact, Napoleon's need to prove himself came from his colossal dong, made all the more huge by his relatively small body. In fact, we get the word *boner* from his last name. Contrary to conventional wisdom, Napoleon wasn't exiled because of his military blunders, but rather because his OMG was discovered by his generals.

Abraham Lincoln

America's sixteenth president was known to suffer bouts of melancholy brought on by his OMG. His wife, Mary Todd, also struggled with mental illness—a byproduct of the stress of her frequent encounters with Abe's horselike genitals. It's also widely accepted that John Wilkes Booth, Lincoln's assassin, didn't shout "Sic semper tyrannis!" ("Thus always to tyrants!") when he leapt to the Ford Theatre's stage, but "Sic semper queerpenus!" ("Thus always to the strange penis!").

Wolfgang Amadeus Mozart

Mozart's obsession with music began at a very young age, when he realized that sitting at a piano helped conceal the massive bulge in his pantaloons. Later in life, he resolved to cut his penis off. His famous "Requiem" was actually composed as a funeral mass for his soon-to-be-severed genitals.

Fortunately, he lacked the nerve to follow through. Mozart's final opera, "The Magic Flute," was an attempt to reconcile with his penis—to forgive it for all the pain it had caused him.

Mark Twain

When a young Samuel Clemens was a steamboat pilot on the Mississippi River, his shipmates used to joke that his penis would reach a depth of "mark twain" (12 feet) if he threw it overboard. The name stuck, though most of his readers never had a clue to its origins. In Twain's masterpiece, *The Adventures of Huckleberry Finn*, scholars believe that Huck's friend Jim (the runaway slave) represents the imprisonment Twain felt because of his huge penis.

How Big Is Huge?

At what point does a penis cease being merely large and cross the threshold into OMG? Beginning with the Canary Islands Conference of 1904 and as recently as Dr. Herbert Sumner's (now widely discredited) *On Huge Penises* of 1970, there have been several attempts to create universal diagnostic guidelines: a certain number of inches, a certain weight, and so on. But these simply weren't practical because penile hugeness is relative to the size of the sufferer, and it can take many different forms. For instance, some penises are exceedingly long but lack girth ("French Breads"), whereas others are quite wide but short ("Tuna Cans"). An OMG diagnosis requires excessive length *and* width; it is usually made in early adolescence, when the defect first presents itself. In addition to a basic visual and manual examination, today's doctors ask seven simple questions to help confirm an OMG diagnosis:

Have you ever pinched your penis under a toilet seat? ☐ YES ☐ NO

Do sexual partners complain of stomachaches during intercourse? ☐ YES ☐ NO

Have you ever experienced numbness in your hands or feet while erect? ☐ YES ☐ NO

Do you buy oversized pants or underwear to accommodate your penis? ☐ YES ☐ NO

Have you ever harbored thoughts of harming your penis? ☐ YES ☐ NO

Can you touch the base of your spine with the tip of your penis? ☐ YES ☐ NO

Generally, if the patient responds "yes" to four or more of these questions, his penis can be classified as "huge."

Leonardo da Vinci

Why is Mona Lisa smiling awkwardly? Because, as Leonardo later recorded in a journal, "that devil had, unbeknownst to me, slithered forth from the safety of my stockings as I painted her." His interest in anatomy came from his need to understand the forces behind his embarrassing growth. And his famous anatomical drawing *Vitruvian Man* was Leonardo's ideal self: a man with an average penis, displaying it without shame. Something the artist was never able to do.

Sigmund Freud

The pain young Freud felt was so severe that he invented modern psychoanalysis to cope with his own troubles. His theory that the desire for sex drives all human behavior is, ironically, a window into his soul, for Freud was sadly never able to experience "normal" sex during his lifetime. His use of a couch during psychoanalysis was considered revolutionary. In reality, Freud found sitting for long periods to be excruciating because of his penis, and he assumed others felt the same way.

P. T. Barnum

Barnum's affinity for "freaks" came from his own experience as a young outcast in Connecticut. Teased and even beaten by his peers because of his OMG, he swore he'd teach them all a lesson by turning his deformity into a fortune. In the end, it was the deformities of others that made him rich. Though Barnum never performed in his own circus, he briefly considered taking the stage with Tom Thumb and having the tiny General do pull-ups on his erect penis—but eventually thought better of it.

Theodore Roosevelt

When Teddy said, "Speak softly and carry a big stick," most of the world thought it was a clever summary of his approach to foreign policy. In fact, the big stick to which he was referring was in his underpants. Roosevelt had spent years carefully crafting a macho image as a hunter, "rough rider," and outdoorsman. But it was all a ruse, a facade to cover up the secret that threatened to undercut his manhood. After leaving office, Roosevelt traveled on safari to Africa, where he vented his frustrations by killing a slew of elephants, rhinos, and buffalo— all creatures with huge penises.

Jim Morrison

In The Doors' "The End," Morrison sings: "The snake is long, seven miles. Ride the snake . . . he's old, and his skin is cold." One need only look at many of Morrison's lyrics and song titles to understand just how deep was his preoccupation with his penis: "Touch Me," "Back Door Man," "Break on Through," and of course "Horse Latitudes." Morrison died alone at age 27, which in 1971 was two years shy of the average OMG sufferer's lifespan.

Sir Winston Churchill

One reason Churchill so vehemently opposed Adolf Hitler's vision of a master race was because he knew he could never be a part of it, thanks to his remarkably bulbous genitals. The Nazis prided themselves on their tiny penises. Hitler himself was said to have a spectacular penis of no more than one inch when fully erect, which he rarely was. Churchill knew that if Hitler succeeded, the world would never be safe for men with average-sized penises, never mind those with OMG.

All God's Creatures, Great and Greater: Huge Penises in Nature

OMG sufferers are often chastised as "freaks" or "God's accidents." But science has made great strides in debunking this old discriminatory rhetoric. A study of dozens of animal species reveals that huge penises are much more common in the animal kingdom than once thought.

Horses Any casual Internet user knows that horses have huge penises. And yet horses are among nature's proudest creatures.

Whales Whale penises can measure up to 8 feet long, which is less impressive when you consider that whale vaginas are often 12 feet deep.

Elephants Elephant penises can reach 6 feet long and weigh more than 60 pounds. Sadly, poachers often kill these creatures to sell their penises as designer sleeping bags.

The Argentine Blue-Billed Duck Males have been observed with 17-inch penises; that's more than twice their average body length. It's the largest penis in the bird kingdom, ever since the extinction of Argentina's three-legged swallow in the early 1900s.

Barnacles Although only a few centimeters in diameter, barnacles have the greatest penis-to-body-size ratio, at 40 to 1. If a barnacle was a 6-foot-tall man, his penis would be 240 feet long, and he would be able to reach the urinals at Wrigley Park from the pitcher's mound.

2

Dealing with
Discrimination

*"Strangers are just friends waiting
to happen."*

—Rod McKuen

DEALING WITH DISCRIMINATION

I n a world struggling to heal the wounds of a racially and ethnically divided past, overhung men are still victimized by what the poet Israel McCarthy calls "the last fashionable prejudice." For a man with OMG, life is a minefield of ridicule, ostracism—even physical attacks. In this chapter, we'll tackle some real-life examples of discrimination shared by your fellow sufferers. After each story, Dr. Richard and Rev. Owen will each present his own view on how the situation could've been handled differently.

Dealing with TEASING

"I was at a Buffy *convention in Denver, and me and some of the other guys (and our friend Emily, who's really cool) were sitting in the hot tub at the motel after a long day of panels. Just your typical 40-something crowd partying it up: eating pizza, discussing all the things we'd ask SMG if we ever met her in real life, and listening to one of my famous Rush mix CDs. So I start climbing out of the tub and suddenly everybody starts freaking out and pointing. I look down, and my cutoff jean shorts have ridden up my leg—exposing the lower half of my penis. 'It looks like a Shai-Hulud!' yelled Pete's friend Chad (a reference to the giant sandworms of Arrakis in Frank Herbert's* Dune*). Everybody in the hot tub started laughing and chanting, "The spice must flow! The spice must flow!" I ran back to my room, crying, packed up my Xander and Willow busts, and took a cab straight to the bus station. I haven't had the nerve to show my face on the* Buffy *circuit since."*

—*Eric G.*

Rev. Owen: When I was growing up on the streets of Brockton, Massachusetts, we had a method for dealing with situations like this. If a group of kids was giving you a hard time, you picked out the biggest, meanest-looking one and cracked him right in the face with a crowbar. After he fell with his nose gushing all over the place, you looked at the other kids and asked, "Anybody else got something to say?" Believe me, they never did.

Dr. Richard: I wouldn't go quite as far as Rev. Owen, but I agree that running away isn't the answer. It only leads to regret ("I wish I'd said . . .") and shame ("I'm such a coward!"). Stand your ground! Ask them what's so horrible about having a body part that's bigger than usual. Would they tease someone with big feet? If they persist, you're probably better off without those so-called "friends," anyway.

Dealing with
MORBID CURIOSITY

"I was at [hospital name redacted pending lawsuit] for my first physical after moving to the area. My new doctor seemed OK at first. He was an older gentleman; midsixties. The exam started off fine, until he lifted my gown to get a look at my testicles. He visibly recoiled, then turned red as he stifled a laugh. 'Would you excuse me?' he asked. He walked out of the examining room, leaving me sitting on the cold paper with my penis dangling. A minute later, he returned with not one, but three nurses and another doctor. I was mortified. 'These, uh . . . these colleagues are here to assist with your physical.' I knew he was lying. They were there to get a glimpse. One by one, they came forward and inspected my penis, each one trying not to laugh. One of the nurses lifted it with her palms to 'check the weight.' Another put a blood pressure cuff around it and pumped it up, giggling like a schoolgirl the whole time. More and more people

streamed into the room—lab techs, administrators, EMTs. It was embarrassing beyond description. When a janitor showed up with a digital camera, I burst into tears."

—*"Omar"*

Rev. Owen: If I had a nickel. "Lookie-loo's" are a constant thorn in my side at the Priest's Lounge in Cambridge. The minute I show up in the steam room, it fills up faster than Fenway Park. When I catch a new guy staring, I usually say something like: "I think your eyes are full. Any room in your ass?" If I catch him again, I solve it Brockton style. Trust me—they have a hard time staring when both their eyes are swollen shut.

Dr. Richard: I disagree. I think it's more important to educate than intimidate. When I find myself in these situations (we've all had that masseuse, beachgoer, or relative that's made us feel uncomfortable), I try to be polite and matter-of-fact. "I see you've noticed that my penis is unusually large.

That's because I have a medical condition called OMG. Don't be afraid—it isn't contagious. I'd be happy to explain more to you."

Dealing with EXCLUSION

"Every year before the homecoming game, my college has this thing called the Parade of Pubes. All these kids strip naked except for their sneakers and run around the football stadium three times. Girls paint mascots on their boobs, guys dress their dicks like the other team's coach, and everybody gets wasted, right? It's awesome. So junior year I'm like 'fuck it.' I'm tired of feeling left out, plus I'm stupid drunk. So when it's time to strip, I take my clothes off. But when my hog comes out, one of my buddies is like, 'Dude, what the fuck?' Everybody starts moving away from me—making a big circle, like they don't want to be near me and stuff. It gets all quiet, and this campus cop comes over to me and he's like, 'Son, I'm gonna need you to put your

clothes back on.' And I'm like, 'Why? Everybody else is naked.' And he's like, 'Son, I don't want any trouble.' And I'm like, 'Fuck you, bro!' So he hand-cuffs me and drags me to the security office. They charged me with public indecency for being naked. They even took away my tickets to the game 'cause I was supposedly a 'security risk.' It was totally fascist."

—*Jason D.*

Rev. Owen: Look, it's no fun feeling left out, but there's also something to be said for picking your battles. Personally, I wouldn't have gotten naked in front of a whole crowd of college kids. Seems to me like you were asking for trouble. One of my cardinal rules is, Never show your penis to more people than you're prepared to fight.

Dr. Richard: The Reverend and I are on the same page here. Confronting prejudice is most effective when it's done one person at a time. When you feel excluded, the first thing you need to do is give yourself a shot of vitamin E ("e" for "esteem"). Remind yourself it's their ignorance that's at fault, not your huge penis. Otherwise you run the risk of losing your temper.

Dealing with FEAR

"We'd just finished dinner. I'll never forget the amount: $366.68. Not because it was a lot to spend on dinner for two, but because of the 666 in the middle. One of those things that gives you a chill when you think about it later. Anyway, I paid, got her coat from the checkroom, and walked her to the car. In the parking lot, while I was punching the address of this club into the navigation system, she said, 'I want to thank you for dinner,' and started rubbing her hand on my leg. 'Right here?' I asked. 'Right here.' She started undoing my zipper, and I thought, should I say something? But it was too late. Out it came. She jumped back and shrieked—turned and frantically started pulling the

door handle, but the automatic locks were on. She took off her Rolex, hyperventilating. 'Please! Please don't kill me! Take anything you want!' She dug through her purse and threw her wallet at me. I just sat there, stunned. Paralyzed with confusion. The next thing I knew, she pepper-sprayed me in the face. I screamed, clutching my eyes and dry heaving. She finally got the door open and ran off into the night."

—"DK"

Rev. Owen: Well, I'd say the relationship was doomed from the get-go. I mean, unless you were planning to follow in my footsteps and choose a life of celibacy, she was going to see your penis sooner or later. Better to get it over with and save yourself another pricey meal. In fact, if you'd brought up your OMG during dinner, you might've gotten away with nothing more than a glass of wine in the face.

Dr. Richard: Remember that moment where you

wondered whether you should say something? Well, you probably should have. Unfortunately, we overhung men have to be extra cautious. We have to assume that people will be frightened when they first lay eyes on our genitals. Sure, it's unfair that we're persecuted for having thick, meaty penises, but it's equally unfair to take someone by surprise with them.

Dealing with THREATS OF PHYSICAL VIOLENCE

"We were pinned down on a rooftop in southeast Fallujah, and the mortar rounds were getting closer and closer. There was no time to wait for the armor to show up—we had to put some lead on these motherfuckers before they dialed us in. Sarge ordered me to lay down a suppressing fire. I crossed myself, stood up, and started spraying. An instant later, a sniper put a round right through my thigh. I fell back, clutching my leg. Doc was there

right away. 'Lay still!' I felt the needle go in. I felt the scissors cut away my fatigues. I remember seeing a bunch of jaws drop, and somebody yelling, 'Holy shit! He's a fucking hoco!' [See "Hurtful Huge Penis Slurs," page 67.] Sarge tried to pull the Doc off me, and yelled, 'Let the fucker bleed out!' 'No! I took an oath, dammit!' The other guys in my unit gathered behind Sarge and pointed their rifles at me. 'Let me shoot him, Sarge!' 'Fuck that, let me!' Sarge drew his sidearm and pointed it at Doc's head. 'Now I'm gonna count to thr—' But before he could finish, a mortar hit the roof dead center. The next thing I remember is waking up in a hospital bed in Germany."

—"Ernesto"

Rev. Owen: I don't even know what to say to this. I've read your story over and over, looking for some lesson to take from it. Something positive. But all it does is reinforce my fear that everything I've done with my life—trying to spread Christ's message of charity and tolerance—has been in vain. The older I get, the more I think we're nothing but a bunch of animals, and that we deserve whatever God throws our way.

Dr. Richard: Once again, I disagree with my friend. I think the fact that Doc wanted to help you in spite of your OMG shows the tremendous progress we've made in the last hundred years. As for what I would've done differently: I might've tried to add a calming voice to the chaos instead of sitting there silently. "Hey guys, I see you've noticed that my penis is unusually large. That's because I have a medical condition called OMG."

"COBRA," BY ISRAEL McCARTHY

Born in 1934 on the Amalfi Coast, Israel McCarthy ran away to London as a teenager and took a job as a cab driver's apprentice while he attended night classes at the English Academy of Poetry. In 1955 he set the beat movement on fire when he published his first collection, "Poems About My Huge Penis." Since then, he's devoted his life and career to the issues faced by men with OMG: holding charity events, speaking at campuses across the world, even creating a line of specialty pants. But his greatest contribution to our cause has been his body of work—hundreds of poems about the struggles of having a huge penis. One of the very best is "Cobra," from his first collection.

Cobra
That cobra is everywhere, man,
Poised to bite,
Poised to bite,

At night the venom pours from his toothless
mouth,

Weaving a silken blanket that warms my chest,

A lover's bed without a guest,

I wipe his mouth,

A gentle kiss,

His glistening lips,

His eyeless face,

An artist's dream,

But not mine, man,

Not mine.

CHAPTER

3

Unzipping: Coming Out to Your Friends and Family

"If you reveal your secrets to the wind, you should not blame the wind for revealing them to the trees."

—*Kahlil Gibran*

A man cannot truly *live* with a huge penis if he's forced to keep it hidden from those closest to him. As frightening as it may seem in our OMG-phobic world, coming out is a crucial step on the road to the "normal" life most overhung men crave. But it's not something that should be rushed into, since choosing the wrong time or methods for revealing your big secret could have tragic consequences. In this chapter, we'll offer some ways to make your own unzipping as painless as possible and share some coming-out stories from other sufferers.

The following story illustrates how *not* to come out to your loved ones:

Christmas morning, 1983. The O'Donnell family rose early to open presents and snuggle around the fireplace of their old Massachusetts farmhouse: Bill and Maggie, their kids Mary, Katie, Sean, twins Frank and Aiden, Megan, Pete, baby Molly, and Bill Jr.—the eldest, home from his first semester of college. Unbeknownst to his parents and siblings, Bill Jr. had decided to share his secret with the whole family in dramatic fashion, hoping the holiday spirit would ease their shock. When it came time for him to open his stocking, Bill Jr. pulled it off his lap, revealing his massive penis—to which he'd affixed a bow.

"My father walked calmly out of the room as my mom, brothers, and sisters cried. When he came back, he had his old Remington 12-gauge. I thought he was going to shoot me—we all thought so. Instead, he just sat down in his favorite leather recliner, muttered 'Merry Christmas,' and blew his brains out."

It's an all-too-common result, but it doesn't have to be . . .

Be Prepared

Pick the Right Time

Although every unzipping is different, there are a few universal truths that all men with huge penises would do well to remember:

Don't Unzip in Anger. Some men make the mistake of whipping out their cookie dough in the heat of an argument, something Rev. Thomas calls the "Oh yeah?" moment: "Oh yeah? You don't think I try hard enough in school? Try sitting at a desk all day with *this*!" or "Oh yeah? So now I'm an alcoholic? Let me ask you a question: Would you drink if you were born with *this*?" Throwing your massive genitals into an argument is like throwing dynamite on a campfire.

Gauge Overall Stress Levels. The happier and more relaxed your intended targets are, the better. If you're planning on unzipping to your parents, doing it while they're in the midst of a bankruptcy might not be the way to go. Likewise, if your buddy is going through a bitter breakup, you should probably take a rain check on showing him your giant penis.

Avoid Holidays. Young Bill O'Donnell learned this one the hard way, but he's not alone. Many OMG sufferers try to soften the impact by coming out on a holiday—putting a sparkler in their urethra on the Fourth of July; dressing up as an anatomically correct horse for Halloween; dyeing their penis for Easter. It never works. Unzipping is dramatic enough; adding the drama of a festive occasion only makes things worse.

Pick the Right Setting

Assuming you've picked a time when friends or loved ones are upbeat and relaxed, you'll need to pick a setting to match.

Avoid Public Places. Men with OMG are often tempted to unzip in public as "insurance" against excessive outbursts or violence. But doing so can have the opposite effect—intensifying a friend's or relative's embarrassment and triggering a psychotic episode (see "Uncontrollable Rage," page 56).

Prescreen the Environment. Once you've settled on a quiet, private location, you should screen it ahead of time, even if it's a place as familiar as the family living room. Stand in the space and visualize your unzipping. Carefully note all exits. Remove anything that might be used as a weapon.

Avoid "Kill Triggers." Your setting should be free of anything that might inflame an already-tense situation and trigger the primal urge to kill: family photos from happier times, an abundance of the color red, or anything that bears even the slightest resemblance to a huge penis (fire extinguishers, grandfather clocks, short-hair Daschunds, etc.).

Bring Backup

Things are likely to get contentious—even violent—

during your unzipping. It's always good to have someone in your corner.

A Friend. Obviously, one who already knows your secret and has accepted you as a fellow human being in spite of it.

A Fellow OMG Sufferer. Whether he's from your support group or just someone you found on one of the many Internet message boards for overhung men. It's an added bonus if he's already been through his own unzipping and knows what to expect.

A Clergyperson. If, that is, they're willing to help. Sadly, there are still very few priests, rabbis, or imams who will counsel men with huge penises.

Be Gentle

Before You Tell
Set the Mood. Ask everyone to sit. Speak in a soft,

even voice. Make sure everyone has used the rest-room and ask that all phones be turned off. (Keep yours on silent, just in case you need to call 911.)

Start with an Affirmation. Tell your family how important they are to you and that for a long time you've been anxious to share something painful with them. Tell them that no matter what happens in the next few minutes, hours, or weeks, you'll always love them. (NOTE: At this point in the unzip-ping, most friends and relatives will assume you're about to come out as a homosexual. It's best to move through this confusion quickly to minimize their disappointment when they learn you aren't).

Lend Some Perspective. If your family is religious, ask them if they think God created man in his own image. If they're secular, ask them if they agree with the American ideal of "all men are created equal." Ask them if they admire people like Albert Einstein and Abe Lincoln. (NOTE: Now they're *sure* you're about to come out as gay. Hurry up and get to the point).

Tell the Truth. Announce the following in a loud, clear voice: "_____, I have a condition called Oversized Male Genitalia."

After You Tell

Realize They'll Be Shocked. Gasps and tears will probably drown out the words *male genitalia*. Once they hear *oversized*, they'll be swept away to a land of nightmares where warmth, love, and beauty can't find them. Preconceptions and fears will fly around their heads like bats in a burning barn. Some will vomit. All will cry. A few may even lunge at you before the phrase has fully left your tongue. Remember, unless you grew up in Japan, your parents haven't seen your penis since adolescence. The same is true for friends and siblings. Therefore, they probably had no idea you were suffering from OMG.

Stay Calm. Short of protecting yourself from physical attacks or ducking to avoid flying objects, it's crucial that you remain perfectly quiet and still during this initial reaction. Let your family work through it. Let them cry, scream, and curse God.

Do *Not* Show Them Your Penis. Some men feel compelled to follow up their confession with an immediate display of their huge penis—as if to emphasize a closing argument by holding up the one piece of irrefutable evidence. But this isn't *Law & Order*. Showing them your offending member will only intensify their shock and anger. Even if they *ask* to see it, politely decline. (They're almost always asking to "see it" so they can attack it.)

Know What to Expect

"Anakin" (real name withheld for his own protection) was 17 when he unzipped to his mother, father, and younger brother. His story is about as typical as they come, and it serves as the perfect way to illustrate the six stages that your friends and family are likely to go through:

1. Denial
2. Uncontrollable Rage
3. Mourning
4. More Uncontrollable Rage
5. Banishment
6. Acceptance

Remember: Each stage can take anywhere from a day to a decade to work through, and not everyone experiences them all.

Stage One: Denial

"It was like she hadn't heard a thing I said. 'Mom,' I repeated, 'what are you doing?' 'What does it look like I'm doing, dear? I'm fixing dinner. My boys need to eat, don't they? We'll just sit around the table and have a nice dinner tonight. The four of us, all together.' My little brother had slammed his door and cranked up his Bon Jovi. Dad had left to go to a friend's house and get drunk. And here was my mother—making a meatloaf, as if nothing had happened. 'Mom, I have OMG.' 'Should we have spinach or mashed potatoes?' 'Mom! I have an oversized penis!' 'You know what? Let's have both, just to be on the safe side. We can always save the leftovers.'"

Stage Two: Uncontrollable Rage

"Things got out of control when Dad came home absolutely plastered. Mom had been sitting in the dining room by herself watching dinner get cold for hours. My brother hadn't shown his face. Dad was actually laughing when he walked in, carrying a brown paper bag. 'Hey! I got us some groceries!' he said, slurring his words. I met him in the foyer. 'Dad, I love you. We need to talk about this.' 'Look!' He pulled an unwrapped pork loin out of the bag. His expression changed. 'I thought you'd like it, you goddamn freak!' What happened next is a blur. All I remember is Dad mercilessly beating me about the head and neck with the loin. I remember Mom screaming in the next room and throwing serving dishes against the wall. I remember my brother rushing to my aid, shrieking, 'He's still your son! He's still your son!' Then everything went dark."

Stage Three: Mourning

"After hours of screaming and crying, I thought the worst was over. Everyone had finally gone to bed around one in the morning. At three, unable to sleep, I went downstairs to grab a glass of water. But when I opened the fridge, I heard a noise in the darkness. I turned and saw the shadowy outline of my father on the kitchen floor. He was just sitting there, holding his knees tightly against his chest, rocking back and forth and whispering over and over, 'My son is dead . . . my son is dead . . . oh my God . . . oh my God.' When I turned on the lights, I saw that he was sitting in a puddle of his own urine. 'Dad?' I asked. He looked right at me, his face caked with dried tears, and asked, 'Did you know my son? He was a good boy, wasn't he?'"

Stage Four: More Uncontrollable Rage

"Two full days passed without incident. We all went about our business. Dad went to work. Mom cooked and cleaned. My brother and I went to school. No one said a word. On the third night, we gathered around the dinner table and ate greasy chicken out of a bucket—the four of us staring at our plates the whole time. My brother's soft voice finally broke the silence: 'Mom, can you please pass the—' Dad dove across the table and punched him in the mouth, knocking him off his chair. He kept pummeling my brother, even as I tried to pull him off. The three of us rolled across the floor—kicking, punching, and choking each other. Out of the corner of my eye, I saw Mom climb onto the table and begin tearing off her clothes. When my brother and I finally managed to subdue Dad, we looked up and saw her on the table—pulling out clumps of her hair, completely naked."

Stage Five: Banishment

"The three of us sat in the living room. Mom was

up and walking by this time. 'Your mother and I have decided to cut you off,' Dad began. There'd be no more car payments. No more health insurance. No college tuition. I was out of the will. Out of the family. They never wanted to see or hear from me again. 'We don't approve of your lifestyle, and we sure as hell don't want you around our grandkids when your brother gets married.' They acted like I'd chosen this curse. Chosen to have a third arm draped over my balls. I know I should've argued, begged them to reconsider. But all I could do was burst into tears. I just didn't have any strength left. I stood up, walked to the door, and said, 'I'm sorry I turned out to be such a disappointment. If it means anything, I still love you.' I saw my father's eyes moisten. 'I know, son. Just—just go.' With that I left, not knowing that I would never see him again."

Stage Six: Acceptance

"I hadn't seen my family for months, except the night my brother met me at a convenience store to give me some winter clothes. Living out of my car was getting harder as the weather turned cold, and I'd been turned away at the shelter run by our family pastor. I took to petty theft to survive. When I couldn't steal enough to eat, I was forced to give $4 handjobs in the alley behind the Dairy Queen. Thoughts of suicide crept in. And then, one morning, I woke to a knock on my windshield. It was my brother. 'Dad's dead.' The doctors said it was a massive heart attack brought on by high cholesterol, obesity, and a lifetime of smoking. But I knew what he'd really died of—shame. Today, Mom's medications are keeping her up and about, my brother is almost finished with his parole, and I'm working 20 hours a week at the same D.Q. behind which I used to service johns. Life is fun again. The future is bright again. And I wouldn't have any of it if I hadn't had the courage to unzip."*

----

*The vast majority of friends and family never reach this stage. "Anakin" acknowledges that he's one of the fortunate few.

Fun with Your Huge Penis #1:
"Sirloin or Penis?"

A laugh-a-minute party game in which blind-folded players have to guess—based solely on sound—whether various objects are being smacked with either your huge penis or an uncooked sirloin steak.

What You'll Need:
2–6 players (who are aware of your OMG and comfortable with it)
1 raw sirloin steak (16 oz or more)
1 huge penis
blindfold
kitchen timer or stopwatch

How to Play: Players divide into teams of two and "rock, paper, scissors" to determine the order of turns. On each team, one member is designated as the "guesser," and the other is the "smacker." During each turn, the guesser is blindfolded, and the smacker chooses either (a) the sirloin or (b) the huge penis, plus a nearby object to smack it with. Objects can be virtually anything in sight: a countertop, a drinking glass, another player's cheek, a family pet, etc. The smacker announces what the object is, then smacks it (only once). The other players immediately shout, "Sirloin or penis?" The guesser then has 30 seconds to render a verdict based on the sound. No clues or re-smacks are permitted. Each correct guess counts as one point. The first team to ten points wins.

4

Care and Maintenance of Your Huge Penis

"Health is worth more than learning."

—*Thomas Jefferson*

S pecial things require special care. Unfortunately, thanks to our current climate of fear and prejudice, many OMG sufferers are never taught the proper grooming, moisturizing, and massaging techniques that are so essential to maintaining huge-penis health. Instead, they grow up treating their penises as if they were average sized—a slight that can lead to severe complications later. Having a huge penis is hard enough. Having a huge, unhealthy penis is more than any man should have to bear.

Common Health Concerns

Drainage Because the OMG urethra (commonly referred to as the "pee hole" or "wee-wee tunnel") is so long, fluids may not adequately drain from it. This can lead to a terrible condition called Maury Povich Syndrome, in which the entire body begins to emit a strong odor of stale urine. Likewise, if you fail to remove lingering ejaculate from the urethra of a huge penis, it could harden into a cementlike substance called "cumcrete." If that happens, you'll have to go to the emergency room and have your urethra re-drilled, an excruciating, embarrassing procedure. To avoid these problems, always shake vigorously after urinating or ejaculating and follow up with a "toothpaste squeeze," making a ring around the base of your penis with your thumb and index finger and slowly sliding it up the shaft as you would a tube of toothpaste.

Foreskin Irrigation Circumcision is common in many parts of the West, but the vast majority of the world's OMG sufferers are uncircumcised. Their penises are topped with absurdly large, fleshy hats of foreskin that cover the urethra, creating a warm, moist breeding ground for bacteria and acting as tiny vacuums sucking up dust and dirt. If left alone, this problem can lead to terrible conditions such as Cannoli Penis, in which massive amounts of foamy pus collect in the foreskin. It can also lead to Tumbleweeds, little balls of dust, lint, and dirt that form on the tip of the penis, making urination extremely difficult. To prevent these and other conditions, the foreskin should be pulled back and irrigated once a day with warm, slightly soapy water. This procedure is made easier by using a sport bottle or turkey baster.

Shaft Rolling The interior of the penis is made up of spongy tissue that expands when filled with blood to produce an erection. Men with huge penises have a harder time achieving and maintaining erections than "normal" men, simply because their penises require so much more blood to fill the void. Therefore, keeping your spongy tissue healthy and free of clots is essential. The best way is through "shaft rolling." Once a week, place your penis on a flat surface and gently go over it with a rolling pin (the heavy, marble ones work best), back and forth, about ten times. This will also help prevent the big, bulging veins that plague so many of our brothers. Besides being unsightly and mildly uncomfortable, those veins have been known to burst during intercourse, which can be extremely traumatic for everyone involved.

Hurtful Huge Penis Slurs

HOCO A derogatory term for a man with a huge penis and an abbreviation of "horse cock." Easily the most common anti-OMG slur, its roots date back to the Civil War South, where a reporter for the *Birmingham Lantern* once described Abe Lincoln as "that long-legged, horse cock'd scoundrel."

Example: *"I heard that Russ from accounting is a closet hoco."*

LOUIE Another derogatory term for an OMG sufferer and an allusion to "Louisville slugger," the world-famous brand of baseball bats. The slur first gained popularity on the minor league circuits of the 1930s but didn't reach the mainstream until Richard Berry immortalized it two decades later in the classic rock song "Louie Louie."

Example: *"Don't you ever call my sister again, you filthy Louie!"*

POOH'S ARM "Something that always gets stuck in the honey pot." A derogatory term for an over-sized penis and a reference to Winnie the Pooh, the popular children's character. To our knowledge, Pooh's creator, A. A. Milne, was not afflicted with OMG.

Example: *"The guy had a Pooh's arm! It was disgusting!"*

Proper Undergarments Men with huge penises have no business wearing "tighty whities," boxer briefs, or any undergarment made with synthetic fibers. Wearing any of these is akin to throwing your penis in a prison cell and sentencing it to life without parole. Your shaft rubbing raw against its polyester bars. Your head strangled by its tight elastic. Your balls yearning to be free. Boxer shorts are the only healthy undergarments for men with OMG—and only if they're made of either 100 percent cotton or silk. It's also recommended that you buy one size too large (if you're an L, buy an XL, and so on). This will reduce your overall discomfort and help prevent long-term friction and blood-flow-related injuries. You wouldn't put a lion in a hamster cage, so why would you stuff a huge penis into an average man's underwear?

Rod Rash When you have a weapons-grade wang, the occasional penile wound is a fact of life. Every OMG sufferer over the age of 20 can tell you stories of sitting on his penis, slamming it in a car door, getting it caught in a pool filter, or waking up to find the family cat using it as a scratching post.

Most of these injuries should be treated exactly as you'd treat them on any other appendage. But the most common wound experienced by overhung men requires special care: "Rod rash" is the raw, inflamed penile skin caused by excessive sexual friction. After sex (or intense masturbation), if you find that your penis looks like the inside-out baboon from *The Fly*, or that the slightest movement of air over your penis makes you nauseous with pain, you'll need to act quickly:

- Soak three feet of gauze in liquid vitamin E.
- Pour hydrogen peroxide on the affected areas (this will hurt).
- Allow your penis to air dry.
- Apply antibiotic ointment to the affected areas (this will also hurt).
- Wrap the wet gauze around your penis (this will really hurt).
- Keep your penis elevated and well ventilated for six hours.

Penile Skin Care To minimize the frequency of rod rash and other common penile skin conditions (such as penile dandruff, which can fall down your pant legs and result in embarrassing flakes on your shoes), it's essential to maintain proper penis moisture, especially during the dry winter months. Be sure to apply a liberal amount of skin lotion to your penis at least once a day. It's also important to use sunscreen with an SPF of 30 or higher when you expose your penis to direct sunlight. Unprotected exposure can lead to **leather loin,** a heavily sun-damaged penis that looks like an old cowboy boot. Above all, just practice good penile hygiene. Remember, "normal" men can go for days without showering or scrubbing their genitals, but since our penises are so much bigger (and give off so much more heat), we're at higher risk for **swamp crotch,** a condition in which bacteria begin to colonize the creases of our balls and make our privates smell like the Louisiana bayou on a sweltering summer's day.

Surgery: To Chop or Not to Chop

It's a question that every man with OMG confronts at some point: Should I have the surgery? For the vast majority of sufferers (including both of your humble authors), the answer is no—usually because of fear, the enormous cost of the procedure, or, in our case, personal pride. In fact, we debated whether to include this section at all. There's a growing feeling in the OMG community that surgery is an insult to all sufferers—what Dr. Herbert Sumner called "the coward's way out." (Ironically, after his death in 1986, it was revealed that Sumner himself had elected to have the surgery, further discrediting his work.) In the end, we decided to offer two opposing arguments and leave the choice to you.

Pro: *"Jeremy" is a custom motorcycle fabricator who had the surgery in 2002.*

"Would I do anything differently? Not a chance. Yes, the surgery was excruciating, and the two years of recovery were miserable. But the fact is, I have a tiny penis and nobody can take that away from me. I can go to a nude beach without getting beaten up. I can date women without worrying about how they'll react when I pull down my pants. Actually—I can't believe I'm telling you this—but women kind of get off on all the scar tissue. It acts like a natural version of those ribbed condoms, you know? Life is beautiful."

Con: *"Casey" is a Mass tort and product liability attorney who had the surgery in 1996.*

"I call the day I had my surgery 'burial day' because the fact is, I haven't really been alive since. Yes, I had a huge penis, OK? But at least it still resembled a penis. What I have now is more of a Franken-cock. A three-inch nub of flesh that looks like a thumb-shaped quilt. It curves a good 40 degrees to the left, meaning I have to angle my body to the right every time I want to pee. And every time I get to have sex— which is almost never, by the way—I have to attach a football pump to a valve at the base of my shaft since I can't get hard on my own because of all the nerve damage. So yeah, considering the fact that I also went bankrupt paying for all the follow-up care, pretty much the worst decision I ever made."

5

Sharing Your Pain: Sexual Intercourse with a Huge Penis

"When you give yourself, you receive more than you give."

—Antoine de Saint-Exupéry

A ll men with huge penises must hold this truth to be self-evident: They'll never know what it's like to have "normal" sexual intercourse. Yes, it's upsetting. Yes, it's unfair. Get over it.

Dwelling on your sexual limitations is about as useful as a one-armed man crying over the fact that he'll never win a pole-vaulting trophy. Instead of dwelling on being a freak, you need to focus on getting as close to "normal" as you can. And when it comes to sex, an ounce of prevention is worth a pound of penis. In this chapter, we'll start by making you aware of the many hazards of OMG sex. Then we'll walk you through S.P.I.T. (Safe Penile

Intercourse Techniques), a method developed by researchers at Harvard University's Berle Center for Penile Health.

The Dangers of Sex with a Huge Penis

Uterine Encroachment Men with average-sized penises like to brag about going "balls deep" when they're with a woman, but for men with OMG, "balls deep" can lead to deep trouble. Because of their extraordinary length, our penises often extend beyond the vagina, through the cervix, and into the uterus. Accepting full insertion is extremely painful for most partners and can even lead to punctures in the uterine wall, a serious medical emergency. For this reason, it's strongly recommended that men with OMG do *not* have vaginal sex with a pregnant partner, for it could be traumatizing or even physically harmful to the fetus. Almost all cases of adult phallophobia (the unnatural fear of penises) are the result of a frightening encounter with a huge penis while in the womb.

Faintness or Death Because of the vast amount of blood required to produce an erection in a huge penis, men with OMG—particularly smaller, skinnier men—should immediately cease sexual activity if they experience any of the following:

- Numbness in the hands or feet
- Dizziness, blurred vision, or confusion
- Hallucinations (particularly those of talking animals)

These could all be signs of a serious lack of blood flow to the brain, and if ignored, could even lead to death. If these symptoms occur, you need to reduce your erection as quickly as possible. (Many overhung men carry pictures of their deceased pets or grandfathers in their wallets for this purpose.) If this faintness occurs frequently, you should also consider wearing a night guard to prevent nocturnal erections. Too many of our brothers have passed away in their sleep through the ages.

Inadequate Contraception There's an old saying among men with huge penises: the right tool for the right tool. In other words, don't put a queen-sized rubber on your king-sized dong. A fully unrolled over-the-counter condom will only make it halfway down the shaft of most OMG sufferers. Even the so-called extra-large brands are woefully inadequate. And due to the enormous strain on the latex from our massive penises, most "average" condoms usually break before full insertion is achieved. Sponges and spermicidal lubricants aren't very effective, either, since our penises pene-trate deeper than the birth canal. The only reliable means of birth control for OMG couples are the pill and "novelty rubbers," available with a pre-scription in the United States (though we recom-mend buying them online from Mexico to avoid embarrassment at the pharmacy).

Inadequate Lubrication You can never overlubricate a huge penis. Low viscosity not only increases your risk of rod rash but can also cause your partner severe discomfort or medical problems. Under "normal" circumstances, the vagina produces its own natural lubrication. However, when a massive penis is introduced, the vagina, thinking it's under attack by some foreign body, switches into "sandpaper mode" as a means of self-defense. Unfortunately, that only makes things worse for both partners. To counter this natural reaction, you'll need to lather both sets of genitals with a water-based personal lubricant—*not* canola oil or thermal grease compound, no matter what you've read in OMG chat rooms.

Tip Gnawing The human jaw simply isn't designed to accommodate penises like ours. As a result, oral sex can be a painful, frustrating experience. The chief culprit of this misery is "tip gnawing," the inadvertent chewing of our bulbous mushroomlike heads as partners do their best to mimic a "normal" blow job. Even if they manage to take it deeper than head-depth, it's likely that the length of our shaft will trigger their gag reflex. The result? Vomit pours over your penis and shoots out their nostrils, and nobody goes home happy. Unless your partner is a professional sword swallower, it's probably best to leave oral sex off the bedroom menu. Besides, in addition to being unsatisfying, it can also be dangerous. There have been numerous cases in which a slip of the penis has rendered a partner's vocal cords useless.

Sleeving Anal sex is usually off limits, unless you're blessed with a partner of considerable elasticity (in this regard, it's our gay brothers who suffer the most—unable to find any safe harbor for their penises other than a warm pair of hands). Besides the extreme pain of taking a huge penis in the stage door, there are a whole host of medical problems that can arise. One of the most dangerous is sleeving, which occurs when a huge penis pulls the rectum inside out when it's removed from the anus.

Although the protruding portion can usually be stuffed back in by your physician, in extreme cases it may require surgery. Repeated sleeving can lead to **Erickson's Disease** (commonly known as "permafart"), in which your partner's anus can no longer fully close, rendering them incapable of retaining fecal matter and gas.

Organ Shifting No matter how many precautions you take, your huge penis is going to upset the balance of your partner's body. You can't put something that big into an orifice and move it around without knocking into some innards. Your partner may complain of stomachaches, cramps, or nausea during (or shortly after) sex. They may even vomit. This is normal and usually passes after a good night's rest and plenty of fluids. Some partners experience severe diarrhea following sexual intercourse. That is also normal, although they should see a doctor if symptoms last more than three days. In rare cases, the vagina will fail to regain its normal shape, remaining open like a mouth trying to blow a smoke ring. If this persists for more than two hours, call a doctor immediately, since your partner may require Vaginal Botox Therapy.

Fun with Your Huge Penis #2: "Penis Painting"

How many masterpieces can you create with a bit of body paint and a huge penis? Sure, there are the timeless classics like corn on the cob, elephants, and the Washington Monument. But can you think "outside the cocks"? Here are a few ideas from each of us to get your wheels turning:

Dr. Richard's Suggestions:

- **A Lighthouse** Imagine your penis on the sandy shores of Cape Cod, guiding fishermen back to port. Ahoy!
- **Cyrano de Bergerac** The famous Frenchman with the famously long nose. I hope it isn't too runny!

- **Florida** A state that's lovingly referred to as "America's Penis." Paint Miami near your urethra, Orlando on your shaft, and Jacksonville right above your balls!

Reverend Owen's Suggestions:

- **The Red October** The Russian sub from one of my favorite Clancy books. Helluva movie, too—even though I liked Harrison Ford better than what's-his-name. Anyway, paint your dick gray and there you go.

- **A .45 Caliber Bullet** Those things'll put a hole in a man big enough to throw a strike through. Pretty easy to paint, too.

- **The Obelisk in St. Peter's Square** Whenever I visit the Vatican, one of my favorite activities is to sit under the obelisk, smoke a few cigarettes, and people-watch. It's probably a sin to say this, but it's always reminded me of a great big penis.

The S.P.I.T (Safe Penile Intercourse Techniques) Method

Believe it or not, sex can still be enjoyable for you and your partner even though you have a huge penis, and we've combined Harvard's S.P.I.T. recommendations with our own interview to prove it. "Caleb" was a middle-aged divorcé who'd recently started dating a considerably younger woman. His "first time" story is typical.

1. Make Sure Your Partner Is Ready. Deciding to mount a huge penis isn't like deciding to go to bed with a "normal" man. It's a life-changing decision. One your partner will live with for the rest of his or her life. They may want to see their doctor or therapist before making the final decision. Be supportive. Pressuring or "hurrying" them will only hurt both of you in the long run.

"I ran my fingers though her hair. She was trembling, the poor thing. After all the talking, and

planning, and dry runs, this was it. It was finally going to happen. Abby [not her real name] had been great about keeping up with her exercise schedule. In three weeks, she'd worked her way up from bratwurst, to cucumbers, all the way to yellow crookneck squash. I was so proud of her."

2. Let Your Partner Set the Pace. Don't expect to climb on and start pumping. It will take a novice several minutes of slow, steady breathing to accept a good length of your penis. Only after their body has begun to relax can thrusting begin. Some women have likened this stage to giving birth, only with the baby moving back and forth repeatedly.

"On every fifth exhale, I'd gently slide another millimeter or two forward and reapply lube. I was so excited—the time was just flying. When I glanced over at the clock I was stunned to see that almost two hours had passed since I first inserted the head."

3. Be Accepting of Your Partner's Limitations. If your partner is unwilling or unable to do something, drop the subject. Sometimes we have a tendency to project our self-hatred onto others.

"I pushed too hard, I guess, because Abby let a tiny poop go on the sheets. 'Stop, dammit! Stop!' She was mortified. 'I can't do this anymore.' I flew into a rage. It was like I'd been climbing Everest only to be turned back a few meters from the top. 'What the hell do you mean? We just started!' I looked down. My penis wasn't even a third of the way in. Abby started crying again. 'Jesus! This is so stupid!' I yelled."

4. Don't Wait for Them to Finish. Average-sized men tend to wait until their partner reaches orgasm before allowing themselves to. This kind of "penile chivalry" isn't necessary for men with OMG. In most cases, your partner just wants the experience to be over as quickly as possible.

"It was like having sex with the rough side of a dish sponge. Poor Abby—she just wasn't into it after almost four fours of lying there. I kept squirting lube on, but it made things only slightly better. I knew I'd have a nasty case of rod rash on the other side of this, but I didn't care. I was determined to finish. I closed my eyes and called up my emergency fantasy: the old Tina Fey/Kevin Costner/Caleb bisexual three-for-all. It did the trick, as always . . . though I never saw Abby again."

6

Big Blessings

*"Hope is the thing with feathers that
perches in the soul."*

—Emily Dickinson

As men with OMG, we tend to focus on all the things we *can't* do: sit in coach, ride a bicycle, mow the lawn. But, believe it or not, there are actually advantages to having a huge penis. If you look hard enough, there are probably dozens of stories out there in which having a huge penis proved beneficial. After an exhaustive search, we were able to track down four. As always, we'll both offer a brief insight after each.

Cliffhanger

"Back in 1977, I was camping by myself in Yosemite. I used to go there for days at a time to read books, make campfires, freebase a little cocaine—just commune with nature. So one day I'm hiking along a ridge with all my gear, and I hear these screams in the distance. "Help! Help!' Well, I drop my pack and start sprinting. My heart's going extra hard too, because I'm still a little high. Anyway I follow these screams to "El Dedo de Maria," a big, fingerlike rock that juts out over an 800-foot drop. There are three climbers hanging on for dear life out on the tip. I mean, hanging on by their goddamned fingernails. I run out to the end of the rock and reach out my arms. 'Grab on, man!' One of them reaches up and takes my hand, but the other two are slipping fast. They aren't gonna make it. I know there's only one option. With my free hand, I undo my zipper and throw my penis over the side. With both hands, my penis, and the unnatural strength of being high on

rock cocaine, I'm able to pull all three guys to safety at once. If an average guy had been there, one or more of them would've been dead for sure. Today, I'm proud to say that one of those climbers is my ex-brother-in-law."

—*"T-Hawk"*

Rev. Owen: I've never freebased, but one time I was so drunk I put my fist through the window of a squad car and didn't feel it for hours.

Dr. Richard: That was quick thinking, T-Hawk, not to mention extraordinarily brave on two counts: one, the bravery of going out on that ledge to help strangers, and two, opening yourself up to ridicule by exposing your huge penis. Well done!

Case Dismissed

"'Life without the possibility of parole,' they tell me. Can you believe it? Here I am, an old man. Do I

bother anybody? Does an unkind word pass these lips? And what do they do? They drag me out of my apartment like the Gestapo of old. 'We're charging you with sexual assault,' they say. 'Sexual assault?' I say. 'A woman in the neighborhood says you forced yourself on her,' they say. 'Forced myself?' I say. I didn't understand. Me, an old man who never so much as stepped on a cockroach. They tell me an examiner needs to take some photographs of my you-know-what. Imagine the humiliation! Have you ever heard of such a thing? So into a room they take me, and out comes my you-know-what. And all of a sudden these detectives start whispering to one another, and before you know it, they drop the charges and drive me back to Queens. So I say, 'What was that all about?' And they say, 'There's no way you could've been the perpetrator.' And I say, 'Well I know that, but how do you know that?' And they say, 'Gramps, if you'd stuck that thing in our victim, you'd both be in intensive care.' I mean, can you believe it?"

—Abe S.

Rev. Owen: I'm surprised they didn't work you over for having a big dick. Cops are notorious hoco-haters—at least they were when I was in my twenties. I got my share of "whoops-a-daisies" back then. As in "Whoops-a-daisy, our prisoner fell down some stairs and broke his jaw."

Dr. Richard: I'm sorry you had to go through that, but I'm glad everything worked out. It must've been very traumatic, especially for a man of your age.

Big Break

"I'd been treading the boards for two decades, and the closest I'd ever come to having my name in lights was being named 'Waiter of the Month' at the Stage Deli. Sure, I'd been in plenty of choruses, but the only leads I got were in those little off-off-off Broadway fifty-seaters. I thought about giving up, getting a degree, and teaching theater at some high school. Then one day, I see this audition

notice in Backstage: 'MALES 20–35 for the role of JOHN HOLMES in Andrew Lloyd Webber's John! – A new musical about porn and prejudice. Some nudity required.' Well, I was ecstatic. OK, so I'd have to fudge my age a little, big deal. At the audition, all these actors showed up with fake moustaches and stuffed panty hose tied around their waists. When my name was called, I walked out onto that stage (with my real moustache, which I've had since 1983) and pulled off my track pants in one motion. I stood there naked as the day I was born and started belting 'Memories' like my life depended on it. When I finished, I looked out into the darkness and calmly said, 'Mr. Lloyd Webber, you've found your John," not knowing that he wasn't there. But it didn't matter, because I've traded my waiter's apron for a job as the alternate John Holmes understudy in the European touring company of John!"

—Heyward Pryze

Rev. Owen: Whatever.

Dr. Richard: That's terrific, Heyward! I had no idea this musical was even happening! What a tremendous step toward equality for OMG sufferers everywhere! Congratulations on being a part of it, even if you're only a part of it when the two people ahead of you get sick!

Sinking Feeling

"I was sailing my little skiff around Lake Michigan, and the weather was turning nasty. Time to call it a day. But on my way in, a wave sent me smashing into some jagged rocks, punching a hole in the bottom of the boat. I was taking on water fast, and with the wind blowing all over the place, I needed both hands to work the sail. I tried covering the puncture with my foot, but the water just rushed in around it. I was still a good mile from shore, and at this rate I'd sink in a matter of minutes, leaving me to swim in the freezing, turbulent waters. And I wasn't what you'd call a strong swimmer. Then it hit me like a

bolt out of the blue: Timothy! Your penis, Timothy! Of course! I took it out and stuffed it in the hole. The leaking stopped. By the time I got to the marina, the tip of my penis was blue from the cold and bore the nibble marks of several fish. But I was alive, gosh darn it."

—*Timothy G.*

Rev. Owen: Nice work, Gilligan. Hey, here's an idea. Maybe don't go sailing on Lake Michigan by yourself if you're not a strong swimmer.

Dr. Richard: What a great way to use your huge penis! The ingenuity of our brothers continues to amaze me, whether it's a clever penis project, a pair of self-made wide-crotch pants, or a new method of foreskin irrigation. You go, boys!

A Prayer for Owen's Weenie

In my years of ministering to OMG sufferers, I've found that starting and ending each day with a prayer (or affirmation, mantra, or whatever you want to call it) helps some guys cope with the misery of having a huge wang. Eventually, you should try to write your own. In the meantime, go ahead and use mine.

—Rev. Owen Thomas

Lord, I know that you wouldn't create something
unless it was beautiful,
And I know that you created me.
Therefore, I know that I am beautiful.
And because my penis is part of me,
No matter how ridiculously thick and meaty it is,
No matter how many sparrows could perch upon
its endless shaft,
No matter how much it resembles a tube of raw
cookie dough,

I know that yes—my penis is beautiful, too.

*Its extraordinary size represents the extraordinary
love in Your heart.*

*Its burdensome weight is a reminder of temptation's
ceaseless pull.*

*For even though You have given me the ability to
fellate myself,*

*I know that I mustn't succumb to the desire to
do so.*

Even though it would be unbelievably easy,

And no one would ever know.

Except You, Lord.

You would know.

And so I mustn't.

But I could.

Easily.

Oh, Father in Heaven,

Creator of the Universe,

Master of time and space,

Watch over my penis.

Guard it from scorn,

Shield it from shame,

And keep it from getting pinched under the toilet seat.

Oh Lord, grant me the serenity to accept the thing between my legs,

The courage to wear shorts in public,

And the wisdom to shake copiously after urinating.

Amen.

7

Your Daily
Affirmation Journal

*"Your talent is God's gift to you. What you
do with it is your gift back to God."*

—*Anonymous*

A journey of one thousand miles begins with a single step. We hope and pray that this book has been that first step. But, even so, your journey to happiness has only just begun. The rest is up to you, dear brother. The fact is, you will have a huge penis for the rest of your life. Each new day will bring new challenges and doubts. You'll be tested and retested in ways both imagined and unimagined. Your "surthrival" (not just "surviving" but "thriving") depends on maintaining a positive attitude toward your huge penis. To that end, we've included an affirmation journal as a way to greet each morning.

My positive penis thought of the day:

The next person I plan to share my secret with is
_____ because

_____

_____

_____

_____

_____

_____

_____

_____

_____

_____

_____

_____

_____

_____

_____

I am *not* a "freak" because

_____

_____

_____

_____

_____

_____

_____

_____

_____

_____

_____

_____

_____

_____

_____

Hey, I thought of another advantage to having a huge penis! Let me tell you about it.

Here's a drawing of my penis making someone happy.

The next time someone makes fun of my penis, I'm going to say

The next time I feel like harming my penis, I won't, because

My penis reminds me of the following celebrities:

I shouldn't fellate myself today, because

It's okay that my parents don't pick up the phone when I call, because

_____

_____

_____

_____

_____

_____

_____

_____

_____

_____

_____

_____

_____

_____

Some other huge things that God made are

If I have foreskin, the last time I irrigated it was

Besides Kirstie Alley, three people I would *not* want to trade places with are

---

Hey, I made up a joke about my penis! It goes:

It's OK if I never have biological children because

I can't help but smile whenever I think of

A birth defect that's worse than OMG is

_____

_____

_____

_____

_____

_____

_____

_____

_____

_____

_____

_____

_____

_____

_____

Glossary

Canary Islands Conference Held in 1904; the medical community's first attempt to classify OMG as a disease; lasted only two days before descending into chaos.

cannoli penis An infection in which massive amounts of pus and fungus collect in the foreskin, making the penis resemble an Italian dessert; preventable with frequent foreskin irrigation. *See* foreskin irrigation.

Erickson's Disease *See* permafart

foreskin irrigation The daily cleaning of the foreskin with warm, soapy water. *See* cannoli penis *and* tumbleweeds

French Bread A non-OMG penis that has considerable length, but insufficient width.

hoco Derogatory term for a man with a huge penis; an abbreviation of "horse cock."

kill triggers Phallic objects that remind friends and relatives that you have a huge penis, thereby setting off murderous rage.

Louie Derogatory term for a man with a huge penis; a reference to "Louisville Slugger" baseball bats.

Maury Povich Syndrome A condition in which the entire body emits an odor of stale urine; caused by insufficient drainage after urination.

McCarthy, Israel The prominent Italian OMG poet, businessman, and activist.

novelty rubbers Special condoms designed to handle the size and force of a huge penis; available by prescription or online from Mexico.

OMG Initialism of Oversized Male Genitalia, a

genetic birth defect that causes the penis to grow absurdly large.

organ shifting The displacement of your partner's internal organs during sex; can lead to cramps, vomiting, and severe diarrhea.

penile dandruff Flaky penile skin caused by excessive dryness.

Penis Painting A charming and amusing crafts project in which the penis is cleverly incorporated into body painting.

permafart A condition in which the anus can no longer fully close, rendering a person incapable of retaining gas. *See* sleeving

phallophobia The unnatural fear of penises, usually caused by a close encounter with a huge penis as a fetus. *See* uterine encroachment

Pooh's arm Derogatory term for a huge penis, it refers to the popular children's character Winnie the Pooh, that is, "Something that always gets stuck in the honey pot."

rod rash Raw, inflamed penile skin caused by excessive sexual friction.

shaft rolling The weekly use of a marble rolling pin on the penis to prevent clotting in the spongy tissue and to ward off unsightly veins.

S.P.I.T. Acronym for Safe Penile Intercourse Techniques, a method developed by researchers at Harvard's Berle Center for Penile Health.

sandpaper mode The vagina's natural defense mechanism, in which all moisture is sucked out to prevent the penetration of a foreign body; a common reaction to sex with a huge penis.

Sirloin or Penis? A delightful party game in which

players have to guess whether an object is being struck by a huge penis or an uncooked sirloin steak.

sleeving A problem that occurs when a huge penis pulls the rectum inside out as it's removed from the anus; repeated sleeving can lead to permafart. *See* permafart

swamp crotch A condition in which bacteria begin to colonize the creases of the balls, making the genitals smell like the Louisiana bayou on a sweltering summer's day.

tip gnawing The inadvertent chewing of a huge penis's head as a partner tries to mimic a "normal" blow job.

toothpaste squeeze The act of making a ring around the base of your penis with your thumb and index finger and slowly sliding it up the shaft as you would a tube of toothpaste; the recommended method of draining after urination or ejaculation.

tumbleweeds Little balls of dust, lint, and dirt that form on the tip of the penis, making urination extremely difficult; preventable with frequent foreskin irrigation. *See* foreskin irrigation

Tuna Cans Non-OMG penises that have considerable width, but insufficient length.

unzipping The difficult process of "coming out" to your friends and relatives.

uterine encroachment The situation that occurs when a huge penis penetrates through the cervix and into the uterus; can lead to dangerous punctures or fetal trauma.

Vaginal Botox Therapy The preferred treatment for vaginas that fail to regain their original shape after experiencing sex with a huge penis.

About the Authors

Dr. Richard Jacob holds a Ph.D. in Asian economic psychology from East Somerville University, where he also taught until 2003. He lives in Sherman, Connecticut, where he runs an e-commerce consulting business out of a spare bedroom in his home.

Rev. Owen Thomas is an ordained Catholic priest, counselor, and celebrated crime novel author. His Frank Stryver series has sold nearly 90,000 copies to date and has been translated into German. He lives in Cambridge, Massachusetts, and Miami Beach.

Acknowledgments

Dr. Richard Jacob would like to thank

My darling wife, Patty, and our two beautiful children, Huang Li and Liu Hong. Thanks to my co-author, Rev. Owen Thomas (couldn't have done it without you, O). My deepest thanks to everyone at Quirk, the only publisher brave enough to say "yes." In alphabetical order: Bryn Ashburn, David Borgenicht, Joe Borgenicht, Mindy Brown, Brett Cohen, Doogie Horner, Robin Klinger, Margaret McGuire, John J. McGurk, Melissa Monachello, Sarah O'Brien, Lacey Soslow, Lizz Souders, and Mary Ellen Wilson—with a special thank you to Jason Rekulak (we did it, Jason!). Finally, thanks to all the brave men who shared their stories for this book, which I hereby dedicate to my OMG brothers everywhere.

Rev. Owen Thomas would like to thank

First and foremost, God. Without Him, nothing is possible. Thanks to my man Pete at Foxwoods,

Father Frank at Clergy Artists Agency, and all the guys and gals at Quirk (not bad for a bunch of Jews and Eagles fans). This one goes out to all my boys at Charlie Flynn's on Tremont. Next round's on me, fellas.